A POWER of ATTORNEY

LARRY LEVIN

**Executive
Books**

Power of Attorney

Published by
Executive Books
206 West Allen Street
Mechanicsburg, PA 17055

Cover design by Mercy Ehler

ISBN: 0-937539-77-5

LCCN: 2004104785

Printed in the United States of America

Lawrence D. Levin
4 Lawyers Only, LLC
261 Old York Rd. Suite 200
Jenkintown, PA 19046
Tel: 800-681-7000
www.4LawyersOnly.com   Info@4LawyersOnly.com

This book is dedicated to the memory of Albert and Miriam Levin, my parents, who were living examples of the Cycle of Success™. There is no doubt in my mind that their definite major purpose was providing for the family; they were a brilliant master-mind couple; they recognized the existence of the power of infinite intelligence, the universal mind and the ability to think beyond the use of their sensory factors; their never-give-up attitude and their attitude of gratitude still serve me well. This book is also dedicated to the recent fond memory of my brother-in-law, Richard N. Goldstein, who departed this life December 12, 1989, very tragically and much too soon. But within that adversity, I was led to discover the seed of an equivalent benefit, the works of Napoleon Hill and the role they played in Rick's life.

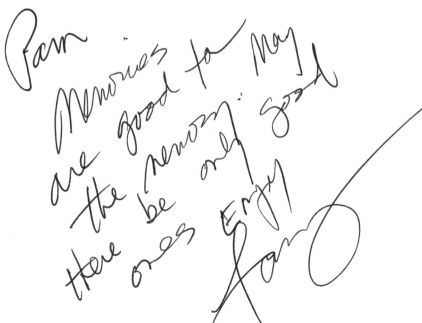

Contents

Foreword

I guess the first time the thought crossed my mind that I might want to write a book was around my freshman year at Pennsylvania State University.It seemed like a cool thing to do at the time; a graduate assistant taught me freshman English in the evening in a loft apartment along with ten to twelve other students. At Pennsylvania State University, this is how they taught freshman English in 1963.

It was going to be the greatest novel ever written. Now, forty years later, I am no closer to writing that novel. Nevertheless, what I think you will find in the pages that follow is my take on a lifetime of study of the *Cycle of Success*™. Success is a science. It has rules that I refer to as universal laws throughout this book. As a lawyer, in the three to four years that it takes to attend law school, we are led to believe that we are trained to "think like lawyers." Sadly, I discovered that we have long since abandoned the thinking process in the legal profession and instead we have substituted "precedent for principle" in our practice of law.

In my view, what we do today, as lawyers, cannot even be considered the practice of "law;" for what we seem to do is to take a problem, find a prior solution in the form of a precedent and then massage that precedent to fit our problem. We seldom, if ever, resort to the creative process.

This was not the case in the past. Some may say that we are thinkers in our profession and in all society, that we use our creative faculties to grasp solutions; but I am afraid that we have abandoned our higher mental faculties and resorted to a stimulus/response, pavlovian process that we refer to as the practice of law.

It is my hope that those of you who take seriously the thoughts that I have shared within these pages and then follow up with the recommended readings, will see that a change in "thinking" is all that is necessary to create a practice that is happiness-centered, fulfilling, and financially rewarding; in that order.

You often hear a colleague say that if only I had this or if only I had that then I would be happy with my practice. What they are doing is putting financial reward before psychic reward, which runs exactly counter to the "Cycle of Success"™.

The psychic income comes first, then the financial reward. It cannot help but follow; it is the natural order of things. This is among the lessons that are taught in *Power of Attorney*.

At the end of the book, I invite you to contact me for an individually crafted "Power of Attorney." This document, which you will execute, will propel you into levels of awareness and successes, both financial and psychic, that perhaps you have only dreamed were possible.

How do I know? My story and my firm's story are set forth in the pages that follow. My background was not predictive of the level of success that I have achieved short of the recognition and then the use of these principles. I have heard others say to me when I have attended seminars or lectures dealing with the "mental sciences;" "science of success;" the "science of personal achievement" that "if I could do it, anyone could do it." These are statements coming from individuals whom I acknowledge later on who came from similar backgrounds as me. Their family pedigrees would not predict what they have accomplished.

You will see that the secret of this success is that you can start right where you are right now regardless of the past, which is powerless to control you unless you let it. My hope is that you will let go of the past, it is not easy, but you can do it. The first step will be to recognize what in the past is controlling you. When you recognize this, you will be thinking, you will be "an observer;" you will actually be paying attention to your thoughts. Your thoughts control everything you do; there is nothing you can do without thinking about it first.

That is the secret of *Power of Attorney*, the ability to recognize the thinking process as it is going on. In most cases, unconsciously at first, but then taking complete control over it. And shaping your destiny in whatever way you choose.

Acknowledgements

Now that I have completed *Power of Attorney*, I must acknowledge those, living and dead, who served as an inspiration, source of information, technical assistance and friends in putting this, what can only be called a guidebook to success, together. First, my main inspiration came from the life, times and works of Napoleon Hill. In *Power of Attorney*, I liberally quote from his best work, *Think and Grow Rich*, but there are several other volumes with which I am familiar and that I have studied over the years that are worth mentioning. They include *Succeed and Grow Rich Through Persuasion*, *The Master-Key to Riches*, *Napoleon Hill's Keys to Success*, *Grow Rich With Peace of Mind* and the book he co-authored with W. Clement Stone, *Success Through a Positive Mental Attitude*.

In addition, Hill accumulated a treatise on success entitled *The Law of Success* which has circled the globe and been translated into many different languages. This volume had a profound effect on the content of these pages. He also produced a home study course with W. Clement Stone entitled *PMA Science of Success*. I also had the benefit of studying several other book and tape courses presented by Stone and Hill. I continue to study them to this day because as I change I see things differently in the way that they were presented by these masters. Napoleon Hill had the foresight in the early '70s to record kinescopes of his *Master-Key to Success* lecture series which now takes the form of a four volume video series. I also wish to acknowledge the personal assistance that I received and continue to receive from Bob Proctor who has authored a worldwide best seller entitled *You Were Born Rich*. He is probably the leading advocate of the Napoleon Hill philosophy alive today. I also have the desire to thank a gentleman who has probably authored more inspirational books than anyone in the world, a recent fond memory, Og Mandino. Among his many inspirational classics with which I have become intimately familiar are *The Return of the Rag Picker*, *The Greatest Success in the World*, *The Greatest Secret in the World* and *The Greatest Mystery in the World*. There are others but perhaps the most influential upon me is *Og Mandino's University of Success*.

Finally, as far as mentors and inspirations go, none have been more influential upon my achievement than Sid Friedman. Sid was my mentor and a close personal friend who has recently departed this world. He, too, was a student of the mental sciences and you will find his thoughts throughout this book. I also have to acknowledge Dale Carnegie, Anthony Robbins, Charles "Tremendous" Jones and all the others whose books, tapes, videos, and seminars have played a role in the shaping of my philosophy.

In the recommended reading list that follows, I certainly hope that you take advantage of some, if not all, of those authors who dedicated their lives to the development and expansion of the science of success.

With the academic credentials aside, now I must turn to those who rendered technical assistance. First and foremost, I would like to acknowledge Frank Freudberg who guided me through the authorship process and without whom this book could not be possible. Thanks also go to my executive assistants who put together some of the notes and typed up part of the transcript with the necessary beginnings and endings. These include Janice Quinto, Eileen Alberto, Pamela Benner as well as the expert staff of Gregory FCA including Gregory Matusky, Timothy Cifelli and Michele Jackson.

I have saved the best for last, though. This could not have been possible without the love, inspiration, hard work, and relentless pursuit of excellence that my wife, Linda, has devoted to this project. It is for her and my children, Jen, Kim and Ben as well as my grandson, Joey, that I pursue these projects. They make it all worthwhile. They are the center of my Definite Major Purpose.

Recommended Readings

The Ultimate Gift, by Jim Stovall
Life Is Tremendous, by Charlie "Tremendous" Jones
How to Win Friends and Influence People, by Dale
    Carnegie
Think and Grow Rich, by Napoleon Hill
The Power of Positive Thinking, by Dr. Norman
    Vincent Peale
As a Man Thinketh, by James Allen
A Message to Garcia, by Elbert Hubbard
That Something, by W.W. Woodbridge
The One Minute Manager, by Ken Blanchard, PhD
    and Spencer Johnson, MD
The 7 Habits of Highly Effective People, by Stephen
    R. Covey
The Greatest Salesman in the World, by Og Mandino
Freedom From Fear, by Mark Matteson
You Were Born Rich, by Bob Proctor
When God Winks, by Squire Rushnell
The Power of Your Subconscious Mind, by Dr.
    Joseph Murphy
Acres of Diamonds, by Russell Conwell
Your Invisible Power, by Genevieve Behrend

Sue Me If I'm Lying

Power of Attorney will change your life.

By buying this book and relying on its advice, we have an offer and a consideration. *Power of Attorney* will suggest that you do things to change the way you see yourself, the way you practice the law, and your entire life.

That is a big promise, and that implies a big disappointment if I am just talking to hear my own voice. Against my publisher's fervent advice, I invite you to sue me if what I tell you does not change your life dramatically—for the better—and if what I tell you is not the truth, the whole truth and nothing but the truth. So help me God.

Power of Attorney is about the 20% of lawyers who make a ton of money, who can't wait to get to work in the morning, who have created comfortable working environments, who have truly cool cases that not only pay fabulously but that are fascinating to work on. These are the ones who long ago have learned to delegate the things they hate to work on and who have learned that when you love what you are doing, it shouldn't even be called work.

In addition, *Power of Attorney* is about the other 80% of attorneys. In this group there are those who hate their offices, who can't stand to think about the mess on their desks. They wake up in the middle of the night thinking about things they did or did not do, thinking about bills they need to pay, cases that they have neglected, and generally wondering about how they got themselves into this position.

Well folks, if you are among the 20%, then read on, because you will see yourself reflected in these pages—and you will enjoy reading about things you are aware of unconsciously, but probably never actively think much about.

On the other hand, if you are among the other 80% (or suspect you are), then read on, too. Unlike the 20% who may read this book as a kind of reminiscence of the wonderful life they have created, you will be reading:

To learn to observe

To understand what makes you do "de-constructive" things

To learn how—using no more energy than you use every day—to start immediately to build the kind of practice (and life) that you have always dreamed of having, instead of the slow, energy-eroding, day-in-and-day-out frustration of sinking slowly in the quicksand of your own frustration and feelings of powerlessness.

So, not only is this book for the successful practitioners of the law, but it is also for those who feel they are always on the verge of breaking through—but who haven't yet figured out how. It is for those ready to make that quantum leap, fueled by the *Power of Attorney*.

Part One

CAUSE OF ACTION

**If you are not now where you want to be,
Your next move is to discover where you really
are, define your dreams and goals, and set into
motion the mechanism to get you there.**

All Modesty Aside
for a Moment

I am a mildly modest man.

However, for just once in this book, I will cast aside my humility and tell you this: I am tremendously successful in the practice of law and in the practice of my life. I built a law firm that has gross sales of $20 million a year. My partners and I built that firm from some very shaky beginnings. For example, our first office was in a converted barbershop where I used to regularly trip over the remnants in the floor where one of the barber chairs used to be. We could not pay rent—but fortunately our proprietor had a host of legal problems and we were able to barter our services for desk space.

Today, people know me as one of the world's pioneer asbestos litigation attorneys. My partners and I practically pioneered TV commercials soliciting personal injury cases. I am just on the other side of fifty, and for the past twenty-five years, people have been telling me I ought to write a book. However, it was not until 2003 that I reached a place in life and in the law where I thought that I would have enough credibility so that the people who could truly benefit from my experience and ideas would take me seriously.

So, if you need help, and if you are willing to spend a few hours with this book and listen to a guy who has definitely gone through what you are going through now, then I believe you will look back on this day and never forget that today, this _____day of_____, 20___ will be the day that you finally began to get what you have always wanted.

As an attorney, I do not make guarantees frivolously. With that in mind, I am telling you that *Power of Attorney* is absolutely, positively, 100% guaranteed to explain, clearly and in plain English, in simple, systematic methods, techniques that I used to get where I am (techniques used by tens of thousands of successful professionals to achieve their place in the sun)—and that are easily transferable to you or to to anyone who seriously wants to learn how to be extraordinarily successful, starting immediately. The ideas contained herein (occasionally I will lapse into legalese. Forgive me.) are not mine. They have literally been around as long as mankind. Mark Twain said, "If you steal something from one man, you are a plagiarist. But if you steal from 100, you are researcher."

Ladies and gentlemen... *I am a researcher!* I have "researched" ideas contained in my book from Aristotle, Napoleon Hill, Moses, the Bible, the Talmud, the Koran, Abraham Lincoln, and St. Thomas Aquinas...

Which Camp Are You In?

If you are among the attorneys who love what they do and who make a lot of money, you will find this book interesting reading—and it will prepare you to attain the next level of success. But if you are one of the too many attorneys who can't stand the situation they find themselves in, you will find *Power of Attorney* essential reading.

You have to ask yourself difficult questions if you want to grow. You have to stretch; you have to find where you are most comfortable and examine what is going on there.

Many attorneys I know complain about "not getting anywhere" or frustration or lack of profitable cases or interesting cases. Nevertheless, when I sit down with them and talk about what they are doing to change things, I usually get a lot of hot air.

What's more, that is a shame, because most of these men and women are great people. Nevertheless, they cannot see that when it comes to growing and changing, they are just going through the motions.

You will not make progress staying in your comfort zone. On the other hand, I am not an adherent to the concept of "No pain, no gain." Why? Because some pain is, without a doubt, going to be part of your life, the no pain, no gain sect confuses pain with suffering. I have a friend active in Alcoholics Anonymous. He says they have a great quote: "Pain is mandatory. Suffering is optional." You will see that sentiment reflected in the pages of *Power of Attorney*. You can suffer if you really want to, but it isn't really required. You do have to stretch a little bit, and sometimes that causes soreness, but that is it. The only pain is the one that comes from building new muscles, not from some kind of cosmic punishment.

I do genuinely believe in, "Stay the same, no gain." However, "What are you going to do with the rest of your life?" Most of us start with plans and dreams and an idea of what our purpose might be, what we want to be, to do and to have. The sad thing is most people give up that idea. They stay in a job working with people they do not like, for money they do not like, doing something they do not like. There is a greater plan for you.

One thing I will show you is how to get into harmony with that plan. Napoleon Hill said, "Somewhere in your makeup, by seeking the seed of achievement which has been aroused and putting it in action, would carry you to heights such as you may never have hoped to attain... Just as the master musician may cause the most beautiful strings of music to pour forth from the strings of a violin, so may you arouse the genius who lies asleep in your brain and cause it to drive you upward to whatever goal you may wish to achieve."

That is beautiful.

That means we all have this wonderful potential inside of us.

We need to bridge the gap and figure out how to get to it. *You do have infinite potential.* Every one of us here on this planet has infinite potential. Infinite, of course, means there is no cap on it. *You can do whatever you want to do.* If you remember anything, remember that. Our goal is to show you how to connect with that infinite potential.

Awakening Geniuses

The practice of law is a thinking person's profession.

We hear all the time that we are trained to "think like lawyers." Yet, thinking like a lawyer has sadly become a lost art. In fact, we as lawyers have confused *mental activity* with thinking.

In this classic treatise, *Think and Grow Rich*, Napoleon Hill wrote about the secrets to success. Professor Hill points out in his philosophy some 17 principles which, if studied and applied, can't help but lead to success beyond your wildest dreams.

Folks, it's that simple!

These 17 success principles are:

1. A positive mental attitude
2. Definiteness of purpose
3. Going the extra mile
4. Accurate thinking
5. Self-discipline
6. The Master Mind
7. Applied faith
8. A pleasing personality
9. Personal initiative
10. Enthusiasm

11.   Controlled attention
12.   Teamwork
13.   Learning from adversity
14.   Creative vision
15.   Budgeting time and money
16.   Sound physical and mental health
17.   Using constant habit force

As we move through *Power of Attorney*, we will discuss some of these ideas, and we will skip some. However, if they resonate with you, and you want to learn more, you now know where you can find them.

In the last few years, as I have been coaching fellow lawyers in the application of these principles, one fact has become clear: as a profession, we are at an extremely low level of awareness when it comes to these principles.

It was not always that way.

In fact, some of the leading scholars and thinkers of the late 19th and 20th centuries were lawyers or members of the judiciary. In the race to "beat the clock"—or bill as much as possible—which has unfortunately become the measuring rod for our professional advice, we have ignored the creative process which used to be the hallmark of the profession. Now we are merely "road warriors" in the race for billable hours; manuscript-like agreements; and instant legal advice.

The art of lawyering is disappearing right before our very eyes.

The success principles that I previously listed are intellectually simple but actually quite challenging to apply. Studying and adopting these principles brings one squarely within the "common denominator" found among all successful individuals, regardless of trade, occupation or profession: very simply stated, that common denominator is that successful people do what failures won't do or don't like to do.

You may ask yourself, "What is it that failures don't like to do?"

In the practice of law (or any other profession), it is the same things that *successful* people do not like to do. However, *they do them anyway*, and they make a habit of doing them. This does not mean that you have to work harder or longer hours or do anything out of the ordinary.

It means that you have to know the truth about what will create success, and then you have to pursue those activities, *even if you do not feel like it.*

That is one worth repeating: even if you do not feel like it.

Document Your Dream

Once you have established *exactly* what you really, really want out of your life and out of your practice of law, create a document.

Call it whatever you want to.

Keep it to one page. Write it in present tense. Consider using graphics, pictures, and clippings to make a collage.

Assign dates to it (this is critical).

Write your plan as if there is no chance of failure.

Be bold.

Visualize your dream in great detail.

If you like, attend programs and training seminars on the subject of how to envision your dream. Do what ever you have to do to capture a clear vision of it. Once you do: print it out on quality paper, take it to a copy shop, and get it laminated. And while you're at it, get another copy reduced to wallet size, and laminate that one, too.

Keep it with you.

Look at it.

Touch it.

Believe it.

Believe it because, as your belief strengthens and your vision crystallizes, the way will be revealed, leaving for you only the need to act on the opportunities.

SUCCESS
FROM THE INSIDE OUT

**People are always ready
to admit a man's ability after he gets there.**

—Bob Edwards

Biting the Hand

Strange as it may seem, I have often heard my colleagues complain that they hate to talk with clients.

Imagine that!

I have even heard derisive comments made about people who help that lawyer earn a living due to the fee generated from that client's misfortune.

Here is the principle. In your relationship with your client, If you "go the extra mile" with a "pleasing personality" good things will happen.

You see, there are universal laws at work here.

These are laws with which we are no longer familiar and ignore to our detriment.

But when I am coaching a lawyer concerning these universal laws, I am able to show how when you apply the law of "reaping and sowing" that the universe will bring you riches in direct proportion to those seeds of goodness you plant.

"As a man soweth, so shall he reap."

Corny?

Yes.

True?

Yes!

Therefore, if you treat clients with genuine love and respect, not as commodities but as "friends," you put yourself in the way of these universal laws, including the

13

"law of differentiation."

This law allows you to stand out from the crowd who treat clients as commodities. If we don't do this, guess what?

Our clients start treating *us* like commodities, as is happening before our very eyes in medicine, and pretty soon we disappear as a profession.

Perhaps you are familiar with the success principles I mentioned. In the example above, I mentioned several of them, including going the extra mile and having a pleasing personality.

All of these principles have been the subject of a great deal of study by the leading thinkers of our society over the last 100 years.

Any analysis of successful people—in virtually all fields—yields a long list of common qualities, most of which are included, in one form or another, on the list of seventeen laws.

Power of Attorney is about applying these laws to the practice of law by first applying them to you.

Men like Napoleon Hill, W. Clement Stone, Dale Carnegie, Dr. Wayne Dyer, Brian Tracy, Dr. Norman Vincent Peale, Og Mandino and many more have written much about these topics. In fact, there is a treatise on the laws of success authored by Napoleon Hill, which he wrote in the 1920s.

I mention these names for a reason: these men have a great deal to teach and spending time reading their books, or listening to tapes made of their books, is time that will pay for itself a thousand times over.

MY FAVORITE IS NAPOLEON HILL'S
THINK AND GROW RICH.

What Do You Know?

We normally think in pictures. For example, if I would ask you to think of your house, you would get a picture of it in your mind's eye.

The same thing goes for your car. It will appear in your mind's eye.

However, when I ask you to think of your *mind*, most people come up with an image of their *brain*.

There is a big difference. The distinction is that we think with our brain—but that the brain is not our mind. (Albert Einstein's brain is on display somewhere in a science museum. Nevertheless, it is just a useless mass of tissue now because Einstein is not with it).

Therefore, if you intend to do some consciousness-changing work in order to become a dramatically more effective attorney, and you want to shift the way in which you think, you have to have a clear picture of your MIND, which is the first step in knowing how the thinking process works.

After all, the power of your thoughts is going to be directed to creating what you want—and to do that well, you have to know how the process works. Otherwise, you are steering your car by watching the rearview mirror.

Once my partners and I became aware of mind technology—how the thought process works—we reduced the time exponentially that it took to create solutions for clients as well as business problems in our practice.

Without that, it was kind of a haphazard thing, but at least we were able to recognize the solution when it appeared. After being able to laser focus our problem-solving efforts, solutions appeared in a fraction of the time. Getting clients, getting referrals, developing winning trial strategies, making fantastic settlements for ten times what we might have originally thought would be a great deal.

INSIDE OUT INSIGHT: in fact, depending upon what the challenge was, we would come up with any number of solutions, and we could choose from the ones that were most profitable. We use these techniques in everything from hiring the right people, making the right choices in marketing, and in selecting or attracting which clients we could actually enjoy representing. The practice became a well-oiled machine, a joyful place to work and a very profitable enterprise—just because we learned the technology of thinking. If you keep doing the same thing, you will continue to get the same result, regardless of your expectation.

If you think that is far-fetched, keep reading.

Anatomy of the Mind

We know that every cell of our being has a biological representation of the mind. What does it look like? Dr. Thurmand Fleet, an American psychiatrist in the 1930s, came up with this diagram:

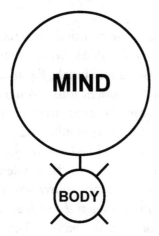

...The large circle represents our mind and the small circle represents our body. Dr. Fleet went on to explain that we can divide our mind in half, and so he bisected the circle.

The top is our thinking (or conscious) mind, and the bottom half is our subconscious (or emotional) mind.

The small circle represents our body with which we act to accomplish whatever results we achieve in life.

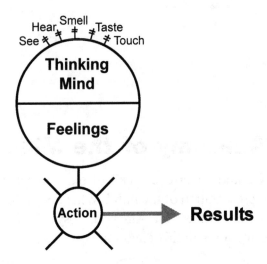

Into the conscious mind, we receive information through our sensory faculties, which include the obvious: seeing, hearing, tasting and touch. Far more powerfully, we receive present-sense impressions through our nonphysical, invisible, intangible "higher mental faculties" which include our memory, our reasoning, our intuition, imagination, perception and will. Many people—but especially most lawyers—are unaware of the existence of these higher mental faculties—let alone know how to use them.

Using the higher mental faculties allows 20% of the lawyers to make 80% of the money. This is no different in any other lifestyle or any other profession. Learning how to use the higher mental faculties allows you to achieve whatever you want—in any realm. Here is how it worked for us:

Instead of just trying to do things better and working harder, like everyone else, we devoted specific periods to out-of-the-office creative thinking; sessions that were so dramatic, they almost felt like out-of-body experiences. At first, they were nothing more than bull sessions. However, soon after we began doing it, something creative would usually come out of them.

By trial and error, we learned to magnify the power of these brainstorming sessions. We raised our own level of awareness.

We would decide who to bring in to the inner circle and how to maintain the appropriate states of mind on a prolonged basis.

The best example of a power idea that came out of one of these sessions was the notion of giving our clients *permission* to refer business to us. I am not being funny.

Now, what does that mean, "permission to give referrals?"

Because of our social and economic upbringing, most of us assumed that it is appropriate to refer friends and acquaintances to other professionals if the occasion should arise. This is not necessarily the case, at least in the field of law that I practice and among our clientele.

They simply do not know that they can refer their friends—that it is okay to do it.

Therefore, by bringing up the subject, by giving them permission, you acknowledge their importance to you, your faith in their judgment, and your gratitude in them expressing their trust in you. That they would share you with a friend is the highest tribute a client could bestow upon you.

INSIDE OUT INSIGHT: Try meeting with five friends sometime in the next 48 hours for the specific purpose of expressing your gratitude for any referrals they may steer your way. Odds are you will wind up with at least one new client—and the sincere appreciation from your friends that you felt comfortable and respectful enough to ask them for their ideas.

That is what happened: we created client friendships and business boomed—and I mean *boomed!* As a result, business immediately became more fun. We actually did a better job because we viewed these folks as our friends, not just as a meal ticket. our minds worked more sharply, the vibrations were there, the legal strategy ideas came into our minds more clearly than before, and there was a very different kind of mindset—an absolutely better mindset.

This new way of thinking—admittedly in its most infantile of stages—allowed us to reach into our higher faculties to nose around for solutions. And the solutions were there!

This mindset makes a huge subliminal impression in the way your clients perceive you and the type of results you get. Your attitude—which you will read about later—is everything, and I mean *everything.* You can be sitting on the deck of a sinking ship, and the right attitude—seeking a wise solution instead of giving in to understandable, reflexive panic—will actually improve your odds of survival dramatically.

We realized there were two types of results we could get just by intentionally tapping into the deeper recesses of our minds.

In fact, the second type was more important than the first. The first was a monetary result, right to the bottom line.

The other was the psychic result, the psychological satisfaction that actually energized us and made us more willing to go the extra mile for the client.

The more willing you are, the better the result.

The more positive energy you give out, the more you attract a like kind.

The more good results, the more clients, the better

you feel, the more effectively your function.

Ladies and gentlemen, introducing... *a vicious cycle of success!*

That is what will happen to you when you tune in and begin using your higher mental faculties.

SUCCESS
FROM THE INSIDE OUT

Learn the art of patience. Apply discipline to your thoughts when they become anxious over the outcome of a goal. Impatience breeds anxiety, fear, discouragement and failure. Patience creates confidence, decisiveness, and a rational outlook, which eventually leads to success.

—Brian Adams

What You Know, What You Do

So now we know that profound changes are possible without some kind of ridiculous pre-dawn to midnight work commitment.

We are at a higher level of awareness, or at least the beginning of a higher level of awareness.

So what?

It is what we *do* that counts.

What we did was become obsessed with learning more about this technology of the mind. The more we learned, the easier it became and the more opportunities presented themselves. We learned to think. We took advantage of some of the personal development programs available. Moreover, we learned from the stick person diagram to quit working on the results and instead to start working on ourselves.

INSIDE OUT INSIGHT: All meaningful change comes from the hard work of altering how you think, the ideas you then attract, and ultimately the physical action you put into it.

What You Want
You Will Get

As you begin to trust your higher mental faculties, you will be inspired to action.

The actions you will be inspired to take will be exactly what you need to do to achieve what it is you really want.

So be careful what you chose to want, they are the results you will attract.

Results that occur will be consistent with what you want. However, that "what you want" part needs intense scrutiny, because often we are confused—without realizing it—about what we really want.

For *us*, one of the hardest things to accept was that what we had been attracting was what we had been wanting.

It all boils down to the power of your subconscious mind and the energy it sends out into the universe.

Those vibrations attract your results.

Baloney? Not at all!

Do I hear someone laughing? Laugh away.

Nevertheless, this is real.

Just like the woman who *always* worries about becoming ill, or the man who *always* loses big in the stock market. They do not *consciously* realize that they are getting exactly what they want—but they *are* getting *exactly* what they want.

One of the most significant losses we experienced was when a founding partner decided to jump ship.

He was a lifelong buddy, a friend, a confidant and a pretty good lawyer. It wasn't until we became familiar with a book by Dr. Joseph Murphy entitled *The Power of Your Subconscious Mind* that we realized that at some level we created the opening for him to make his exit from our firm. Ironically, after an initial period of chaos, the firm was able to break through a barrier that we later could see *he* had created! **Napoleon Hill's principle: learning from adversity.** I swear, when he first left, we had zero idea he was a significant impediment to our success.

His was a barrier of disbelief in the power of thought. Although he was part of our alliance, he remained significantly skeptical—or he would not have left.

However, this exact occurrence permitted us to break through, to quit trying too hard, to let go and let it flow. Now we were able to visualize our success far beyond what we could have achieved with him aboard. This path was available to us. While we were not grateful for his departure when it first occurred, in retrospect, it was maybe the best thing that ever happened to us as an organization.

Panic into chaos into opportunity into wild success.

Go figure.

All Hell Breaks Loose

In 1989, the law firm of Shor, Levin & Weiss had just experienced its best year.

Out of the clear blue sky, one of the Musketeers jumped ship.

My dream of a lifetime partnership with two men I had met at Penn State University was now coming to a puzzling and disturbing end. The surviving partners had no idea why the other one had quit.

So, while we had just divided a seven-figure fee, the Three Musketeers were no more. It looked like Jay Shor and I were just going to have to pick up and start over again. This was not a mere matter of one partner leaving a partnership—this was the annihilation of a dream. I had seen our alliance as almost holy, and this quote from the Bible came to mind: "If one can put a thousand to flight, then two can put ten thousand to flight and a triple-braided cord can never be broken."

We started from scratch many years ago and had achieved remarkable success. Now, one of the basic elements of our professional universe was gone. It felt horrible.

It was our knowledge of the Law of Opposites—a.k.a. The Law of the Silver Lining—that came to our rescue. We knew that on the opposite side of any breakdown is a breakthrough.

Once we got over the initial shock of the destruction of our three-man partnership, we realized that grander days were ahead of us. I did not realize it then, but a silent force had removed itself.

While the departing partner had given what I now knew was only lip service to our success technology—I could now see that he really had no faith in it. Otherwise, he never would have left.

Attitude Isn't Everything, It Is Everything!

"It's the little things you do that can make a big difference. What are you attempting to accomplish? What little thing can you do today that will make you more effective? You are probably only one step away from greatness."

—Bob Proctor

Analyze This!

If you buy no other book as part of your personal growth and success library, you should have Napoleon Hill's *Think and Grow Rich*. You should study this book every single day. The first few times you read it, if you are like me, you will be fascinated by the wisdom—not the knowledge—within its pages.

Moreover, it becomes even more profound the more you study it.

It is a never-ending peeling of layer after layer of revelations about attitude and, ultimately, the principles of success.

I have been reading this book for decades.

The text never changes—but you do, and you gain something with each reading—whether it is a total re-read, or just a couple of pages flipped open at random.

You increase your level of awareness and you see things in a different, brighter, clearer light. I think it's GE that is marketing a light bulb that delivers a more intense range of light waves. Have you ever seen one or had one in your home? It really is a better light. Not brighter necessarily, but it definitely makes things *clearer*.

Well, GE does not offer such a product for the mind. However, tons of valuable books, ideas, and philosophies are out there and they will do the same thing for you.

Keep your eyes open.

Any coach worth his or her salt—no matter what realm he or she practices in—sports, business, science, art—will concentrate on the idea of *attitude*. When a group of people with a common purpose and similar ways of thinking and especially with similar positive mental attitudes get together for a single purpose, the sum of their thinking is a *mastermind*.

The mastermind is an important concept, and we will return to it later. In fact, I will devote an entire chapter to this essential subject.

My partners and I initially thought of it this way: Two lawyers practicing together could earn more than twice as much as one guy practicing alone. We only scratched the surface with that idea. The analogy that Doctor Hill uses is that of a series of batteries. When you connect ten ten-volt batteries, he said, they produce much more energy than the total 100 volts you might expect.

In addition, when you connect minds, you really create something formidable. The power of thought is at the heart of everything that exists.

What do I mean by the idea that *thought* has created everything that there is?

Well, thought power is a form of energy. Moreover, we can summarize the first law of thermodynamics as follows: Energy cannot be created or destroyed, only changed in form.

It is everywhere, omnipresent; and it is the cause and effect of itself.

Now I ought to have your heads spinning by now.

What does all that have to do with the practice of law?

Only everything.

Our profession is one of intellect. We are hucksters, salespersons, and practitioners, whatever you want to call it, of abstract ideas. Thought merchants, wordsmiths, it all happens between our two ears. Once we realize that thoughts are *things*, bits of energy, and once we realize that they physically exist in the universe as ideas, and that we can access it all, then we can achieve anything. Believing this allows you to achieve anything your mind can conceive.

You have heard the expression, "Seeing is believing," right?

I would like to correct the record: "Believing is seeing." Meaning, if you believe you can paint an oil portrait of your spouse, you certainly can. No guarantee as to artistic quality, but if you believe it, you will soon see it. Nevertheless, if you do not believe you can do it, I assure you, you will not do it and, ergo, you will never see it. Ever! See: believing really is seeing. Beliefs are thoughts. They are germs of things. You can nourish those thoughts and grow an oil portrait. It may wind up under a tarp in the shed. Still, what was once a tiny, silly, passing thought can become something which might embarrass your entire family!

If you went out and knew that you had the power to succeed in anything you wanted, I predict that you would approach the practice of law in a completely different method than you do today. My friend, Sid Friedman, likes to ask people, "What would you try if you were utterly, definitely, 100% guaranteed certain that you absolutely couldn't fail?"

I am not sure you, my reader, understand the immensity of that question.

INSIDE OUT INSIGHT: Forgive me if you do under-stand it, but if you don't, please put this book down for a moment and give it some thought. If you could do any-thing—absolutely anything you wanted to do—what would it be? Get a clear picture of it, no matter how unlikely it seems. Get that dream clearly in your head. In Technicolor, get it there in high-resolution HDTV quality. See it unmistakably!

Because by the time you have finished reading this book, I bet you will be wondering, "Hmmmm. Maybe that really isn't so far fetched after all."

INSIDE OUT INSIGHT: However you define it, there is, logically, an original source of all thought. That source would not—and could not—allow you to attract (or con-ceive of) a thought that you are not capable of achieving. This is possibly the single most important concept con-tained in Power of Attorney.

And *that*, my friend is the beginning of nurturing a tiny little brain synapse—an invisible little thought—and building it into something huge. Giant. Something you can take a photograph of: a business, a relationship, a work of art. Maybe even a cup of perfectly brewed tea.

That is your attitude.

That is the first law of thermodynamics.

That is the power of thought. It is invisible, you can-not physically lay your hands on it and you cannot smell it, hear it, or taste it. Nevertheless, it definitely is real. Moreover, coming to believe and understand this is the beginning of learning how to succeed at the practice of law from the inside out.

SUCCESS
FROM THE INSIDE OUT

Success in business requires training, discipline, and hard work. However, if these things do not frighten you, the opportunities are just as great today as they ever were.

—David Rockefeller

While We're Running Around Forgetting How to Be Lawyers...

...The public is forgetting about us.

That is not good.

The public rather expects a lesser degree of quality from us. They have diminished expectations—and we are delivering! We are not disappointing them.

They do not demand more and we give them less.

The relationship has changed from attorney/client to attorney/customer.

Because of ignorance, the legal profession today thinks it should treat a customer differently than a client. However, that was never the case. There is no difference.

A customer is won and done. Find more of 'em.

A client is a deeper, more meaningful, relationship.

We have become like the aluminum siding sales clerk. Close the deal and you will never have to deal with that customer again. Sell them things they do not need, do not want at an exorbitant price and give them nothing free. In addition, give them worthless freebies.

In the past, both parties were part of a professional and caring relationship; they felt like winners in every way.

Remember, relationships give referrals.

The Subject of Bad Jokes, Ridicule...

...and evil characters in movies and on TV.

Do you like what has happened to our reputation?
I do not.

I work hard and love the law.

I am not a sleaze bag and do not like people presuming that I am one.

One of the best character actors of the day, Academy Award winner Al Pacino, was cast as the Devil as a partner in a major metropolitan law firm.

This is a new low.

A big powerful law firm's most seasoned partner.

What did the profession do?

Absolutely nothing. Sat back and took it!

Some say they cast the Devil in an unfair light.

Great!

Are You Broke, Or Close to It?

Are you broke, or close to it? If not, do you have *dramatically* less money than you think you should have by now?

If you are reading this book and you are broke, or having a serious problem with money, I bet you think getting an $80,000 gift of cash—or taking out a giant loan—might help. However, believe me, not only is that *not* the answer, it is another symptom of a serious disease.

Not having money is not the reason you are broke. People think they are broke because they do not have any money. However, they are broke because they do not have the mindset that would give them the money. They think in terms of *lack, inadequate supply, need,* and *not enough.* Thinking that way causes them to act negatively. If they thought in terms of *abundance* and *plenty* they would act as they needed to act to attract what they want or need.

Now if you are an attorney walking around thinking that work is hard, like many people were raised to believe, that it is just too difficult, then you are not going to do things that are congruent with making the kind of money you need to make.

Work can be a lot of fun if you love what you are doing.

How effective are you going to be if you do not

like how you spend your time? The answer is, you are not going to be. Nevertheless, most lawyers are walking around practicing law with that attitude. They really are.

They do not know what they want and therefore, by law, they attract any old thing. What is that saying: *if you do not know where you want to go, it does not matter what path you take.* You have to have a clear picture of what you want. If you do not consciously imagine what you want, you will attract another less-than-exciting attorney/client relationship.

You have to start to change your perception about things. You ought to know what you want. How would your life change if your annual income suddenly became your monthly income?

You should have a clear vision of that. How many lawyers reading this book still have money issues?

Do you know that money issues and your self-image are directly connected? They are tied to beliefs, deep-rooted beliefs, about money.

If you do not have money, you have to ask yourself, "What beliefs do I have that are preventing me from having the money that I deserve?" You deserve to have all the money you want.

Inside Out Insight: This is an extremely powerful thing to do: write down this question in the last paragraph at the top of a yellow legal pad, and then listen to the answers that emerge from that still, small voice inside your self. Write down the answers, and then take appropriate action. Keep writing and listening and taking action and it will be impossible for you to fail, regardless of your age, your obstacles, or where you are when you begin this process.

With the right attitude and the changing legal landscape, a thinking attorney can turn his or her annual income into a monthly income.

What would you do if your annual income suddenly became your monthly income?

How would your life change, and specifically, exactly *what* changes would you make? How are you ever going to get the things that you want if you don't seriously believe you can have those things; or worse, if you don't even know what they are?

We all know that our lives would change dramatically if our annual income suddenly became the amount we earn each month. If I asked you how your life would change, you should be able to tell me, "This, that and the other thing would change. And I'd do this and then I'd do that."

You have to be able to believe it can happen way before you will be able to make it happen.

Your ability to believe has to be cultivated. Start small and, as those beliefs begin to materialize, up the ante. Soon you will be a "no limits" belief machine.

One we begin to believe, our expectation of achievement grows exponentially.

Coincidence?

Have you ever had something happen to you that you thought was a coincidence?

Think back on your life. If, for example, you are married, think back about how you met your spouse.

Many times, it seems as if that was a coincidence.

Squire Rushnell, who was an executive at ABC Television, tells the following story in his book, *When God Winks...*

From an early age, Squire Rushnell knew he wanted to be an announcer on the radio, and there was a disc jockey he idolized, Jack Jones. They never met. Therefore, as he is going through school, he was just an average student who was obsessed with being in that business.

Finally, he gets himself an interview with one of the better New England radio stations, but finds himself somehow without transportation. He has to hitchhike. A beat up piece of junk stops and offers a ride. He is nervous because he does not want to be murdered on the way to his dream interview, but he gets in anyway. He really wants to get to the station without being late.

He opens the door to get in and guess who he sees: Jack Jones!

There's more!

Jones does *not* work with the station where Squire

Rushnell is heading. Nevertheless, Jones takes him to the interview, provides some great tips, and Squire winds up getting the job. This begins his love affair with coincidence and he begins to keep a journal collecting amazing stories.

Squire Rushnell later becomes a major executive at ABC, and becomes a very successful producer of TV shows like *Schoolhouse Rock.*

Fast-forward forty years.

I currently have a national radio show called *A Certain Way.* On it, we discuss the kinds of ideas in *Power of Attorney.* Before I launched my show, I had visualized being on the radio. I had a clear vision of what the studio looked like, the mic, the control board, and the engineers. However, I did not know how to do it. I had no clue. All I had was the vision; and that was plenty.

One day, I am sitting in my kitchen reading a paper my wife reads but that I rarely pick up, the *Jewish Exponent* and I am just flipping through it and find an ad for New World Radio. I call the number and the next thing you know I have a contract to do a radio show about anything I want. Only one problem: I have virtually no idea how to do it.

I took action and made the commitment.

I just knew it was going to work out.

Therefore, I realized I needed a book about how to structure a radio show.

My wife, Linda, and I drove to a big bookstore; we went to the information desk and asked the woman about a book on how to do a radio show.

Her computer showed nothing and she suggested I search the Internet.

Now I have something else I want in this store, totally unrelated to radio production.

I am wandering around and what practically jumps

off the shelf? A book called *When God Winks* (I had never before heard of Squire Rushnell or his book) and I open it up and randomly turn to a page that contains the story about how he got into radio *broadcasting!*

That was the key. I had the clerk searching for *radio* and I gave up.

I did not take the time to think of alternative words with which to search.

Nevertheless, the idea searched for me.

Or was that just coincidence?

Life happens this way whether you are aware of it or not. Just imagine what you can accomplish by taking hold of just this one simple idea.

He Doesn't Have Something In His Eye

What immediately came to mind after I thumbed through *When God Winks* is how often lawyers, who are in the midst of legal research, find themselves down the wrong path because they are simply using the wrong keyword! That is why I counsel sitting down in a quiet place with a paper and pen when you are faced with a serious dilemma. Before you can solve your problem, you have to be able to analyze and define it. Had I done that (not that finding that book was a serious dilemma), I would have realized I needed to redefine my search terms.

So, here I was, having let go of the radio book idea, and then, sixty seconds later, there you have it: the answer appeared before me.

You intellectually let your guard down, and the universe lets the answer in.

By the way, I often say things like, "the universe gives you this" or "the universe provides that." Now, if this kind of talk makes you a bit skeptical, let me tell you that there is no greater skeptic than I.

By *universe* I mean, well... the *universe*. I mean the energy of life. No matter what your religious, spiritual, educational, consciousness philosophy is, I know you do not deny that energy exists. However, if you doubt there is a physical element to the laws of success, first consider this definition:

Energy exists in many forms, such as heat, light, chemical energy, and electrical energy. Energy is the ability to bring about change or to do work. Thermodynamics is the study of energy.

Remember our discussion of the first law of thermodynamics? You can change energy from one form to another, but you cannot create or destroy it.

So, regardless of your beliefs, if you accept the above definitions, then it simply follows that if energy is the ability to bring about change, then thoughts are *literally* energy. Moreover, since energy can never be created or destroyed—only changed in form—then it makes sense to pay very careful attention to your thoughts: where they come from, how you interpret and act on them, and where they go. It is all energy, and in order to succeed, you have to harness it and manage it.

So, when I mention "the universe" do not feel obliged to roll your eyes. This is real stuff, validated through the ages from everyone from Michelangelo and DaVinci to Einstein and Napoleon Hill.

What most lawyers do in trying to solve a personal, legal or business problem is to work from the *outside in.* In other words, they work on the anticipated *results.* However, they never apply any energy to changing anything about *themselves.* They are working under the premise that *they* are not the cause of the results. They believe that circumstance gives them the results, that they have no control over the circumstances—or do they?

Examples:

The judge does not like me.

I do not have enough training to solve this problem. The other side has more money so they will be able to out resource me.

Therefore, what happens is, from that mind-set, they miss all the possibilities to succeed because they have already convinced themselves they *have* to lose! They let the circumstances dictate what they do. These people should read Napoleon Bonaparte (the *other* Napoleon) who once said, "Circumstances? Hell! I *make* the circumstances."

All this takes is a slight shift in thinking: and all of a sudden, you are out of the box of circumstance and into to the universe of solutions.

INSIDE OUT INSIGHT: You open your mind to possibilities that you have not considered because of your mindset. Then, with an open mind, all of sudden, thoughts of a different variety occur to you. You begin to see the possibilities. You look for the possibilities. If you believe you dropped your wallet in the bedroom, you will never look for it in the back of the car. Therefore, it is a grave error to know something—incorrectly.

As lawyers, when we are trying to solve something, we are thinking. Thoughts are at the center of everything we do; we cannot do anything without thinking about it first. Each thought vibrates at a different frequency. The electroencephalogram is able to confirm this. Similar frequencies attract and harmonize with one another. Thoughts of abundance attract ideas of abundance and thoughts of lack attract lack.

Has it ever happened to you, as a lawyer, that you get an idea and ask yourself, "Damn! Where did *that* come from?" It is just the right thing at the right time. You recall a long forgotten legal concept that leads you in the right direction.

Everyone has a perfect memory. Accessing it is the key! When you have something important to work out, but seem to be stuck—I submit that you quit efforting, you let go, and let the universe kick in. You may have some other explanation. Fine! However, do me a favor: Just try these things—like quit efforting. You confidently submit the idea to the universe (or Infinite Intelligence or Universal Mind... whatever you feel comfortable with) and in this case, when you cease efforting... boom! The solution pops up on the screen of your mind.

Part Two

FINDING PRECEDENTS TO SUPPORT YOUR CASE

Identifying and applying universal laws of success propels you toward achieving goals.

Just Floating Around In Space

"Please don't credit me with discovering the Theory of Relativity. I had very little to do with it. It was merely an idea floating in space that somehow filtered down to us through me."

—Albert Einstein

Levin's 72 Principles

...for succeeding at the practice of law from the inside out.

1. Learn About Attitude
2. Study the Laws of Success
3. Read Napoleon Hill's *Think and Grow Rich*
4. Set Goals
5. Divide Obstacles and Conquer
6. Write Your Goals on a Small Piece of Paper—And Keep it With You
7. Never Let Up
8. Identify a Higher Power
9. Don't Complicate Matters
10. Commit to Never Ending Improvement in Your Practice
11. Focus on the Present Moment
12. Keep Journal of Ideas and Thoughts
13. Develop Power of Patience
14. Commit to a Positive Mental Attitude
15. Risk Failing if the Principle is Worth It
16. Get Tough—With Yourself
17. Find Things that Need to be Changed
18. Accept the Things You Cannot Change
19. Change the Things You Can
20. Know the Difference

21. Be Enthusiastic About the Law
22. Help the Little Guy, the Underdog, the New Kid on the Block
23. Acquire the Ability to Rely on Yourself
24. Control Conflict in Your Practice and in the Courtroom
25. Always Try to Settle
26. Listen to Your Instincts
27. Confront Your Fears, Little and Great
28. Seek Progress, Not Perfection
29. Remain Adaptable
30. Think Win-Win
31. Be Decisive
32. Stay Current With Developments in the Law
33. Make Integrity Your Motto
34. Get Balanced and Stay Centered
35. Love Many Things
36. Know Your Flaws, Know Your Beauty
37. Nurture Your Sense of Humor
38. Get Grateful
39. Be Loyal
40. Practice Forgiveness—Start With Yourself
41. Demonstrate Your Love
42. Develop Your Special Legal Talent
43. Be Persistent
44. Develop Winning Habits
45. Do What Other Lawyers Cannot
46. Do Your Work—Even if You Don't Feel Like It
47. Explore What's Outside the Box
48. Neutralize Negative People
49. Catch Yourself Being Negative
50. Catch Someone You Don't Like Doing Something Right
51. Break a Sweat Every Day
52. Relax Your Body
53. Search for a Reason to Have Faith

54. Meditate Daily—However you Define That
55. Remember the Past, Don't Stare at It
56. Consider Tomorrow, Don't Let It Intimidate You
57. Seize the Day
58. Keep Your Business Calendar Immaculate and Accurate
59. Appreciate Your Clients
60. Do Something Nice—Anonymously—for a Judge You Despise
61. Build Networks of Lawyers You Like
62. Build Your Team
63. Take a Lawyer You Hate Out to Lunch—for No Reason
64. Negotiate With Power
65. Always Ask a Lot of Questions
66. Read Biographies
67. Allow Your Opponent to Save Face
68. Make Everyone Feel Important
69. Give Generously
70. Share the Credit
71. Teach Your Children
72. Be a Mentor

It All Begins As a Thought

Power of Attorney contains an idea—a new way of looking at the importance of your thoughts; of recognizing and actually *honoring* the power in them.

It would be difficult if not impossible to name a thing that does not begin in the mind as a thought.

Nevertheless, the weird thing is, most of the time *we do not think*. We just *react*. Even on those rare occasions when we think we are thinking—it turns out to be just another level of *reacting*.

Life in the stimulus-response lane is surviving at the animal level of existence: a low level of awareness.

We exercise little control; we do not know we can control our thoughts and thinking process. It is like the seagull that survives on clams and mussels by picking them off the beach, and then flies over a hard surface and drops them so that their shells will shatter and they can then eat the contents. He knows this works, but he does not know that he knows it, let alone why it works. To the seagull, it is totally irrelevant. Yet, to us—as lawyers, as people, as parents and spouses—it is totally *relevant*.

It's usually an accident when something so profound happens that we realize there actually is some power in the process of deliberately *thinking* in order to create a desired result.

Yet the most successful among us clearly take

advantage of the power of thought and even tell us how and why they are doing it. Then they sit back and observe our utter disbelief in the results and reluctance to imitate for fear of being criticized.

That is an example of Earl Nightingale's observation that the opposite of courage is not fear but *conformity*. We would rather conform than be bold, even if conforming obscures the truth of something from us. All reasonable people know that it is best to conform to the laws of the world, but unreasonable people try to make the world conform to them. Therefore, all progress in the world is due to the actions of those who are, simply, unreasonable.

Does that blow your mind! Does that inspire you to look around in your life for opportunities to be unreasonable? To do things differently, to take chances, to invest in something you believe in? Is being wrong, or laughed at, or humiliated that damn horrible?

In the world, all progress is a result of the unreasonable person.

So maybe, in your life, all progress is the result of the unreasonable thought.

Don't conform to what is reasonable—do what is right.

For many of the unsuccessful attorneys I speak to, it seems that instead of having what they want out of life, they would rather shout about the reasons why they do not have it: blaming the other guy, blaming fate, or circumstance or genetics.

My discovery is that you can have from your practice *whatever* you want—or you can have the *reasons why you do not have it*. It is, literally, your choice.

In my practice, we had good fortune—but only after having ignored opportunity after opportunity to realize that, we could think ourselves rich.

We had to get right with ourselves first.

Why would you think you could choose a business partner with less care than a life partner? If anything, *more* care is required because many of life's pleasures—in fact *most* of life's pleasures—result from your *work*, and not otherwise. My partners and I listened to our instincts, trusted our instincts, believed the little voice within, and then, for some inexplicable reason, chose to give those instincts more credit than they seemed due and then proceeded to see them realized.

It is easy to spend an entire lifetime not knowing what you really, really, really want. It has often been said that the average person, whoever *that* is, lives a life of quiet desperation, tiptoeing quietly through birth, hoping to make it safely to death. As lawyers, we seldom think of what we really want and instead revert to the "party line"—what we have been conditioned to *think* we really want. Moreover, look where this strategy has taken us: right to the bottom of the totem pole of respectable professions.

We ignore our own desires, at our peril, and clients eventually suffer. It is necessary to be practically *obsessed* with our own wants—or we are likely to find ourselves doomed to careers of mediocrity and lack of purpose and direction. We cannot do our best when we are not at our best.

What happens in your practice when you decide what you really want, however, you define that? It becomes crystal clear what needs to be done, what needs to be activated, and what needs to be delegated. You can quiet that obnoxious, doubt-generating little voice from within (the self-critic) and listen with all your being to your non-physical senses.

With that little guy yapping incessantly, it's easy to just tune him out—but at the same time, you inadvertently tune out much valuable insight. You have to go from automatic consciousness to manual consciousness. You have to think about thinking.

We do not realize how complicated a mechanism we are.

Some will say we come with no instructions.

However, that is not true.

The instructions are built in—we just have to learn to access them.

So how do we do that?

Once you really know what you want and you have the belief and expectation that it will come to you, you need only to *learn to improve the way you listen*—and wait for the instructions and opportunity that will soon start to come your way. This requires you to rely on the non-physical: your intuition, your imagination—and quit relying on your physical senses for guidance.

In other words, it is not your job to create a plan; you just follow the one that is set before you.

You do not need to see it or hear it or be able to touch it in order to take advantage of it.

Therefore, if you are saying to yourself that you do not know what you want, I think you are probably saying you are in a state of "not-knowing-how-to-find-out" what you want.

It is in there, believe me, it is in there—but you may be unaware of how to access it, in a prison of unawareness. I do not mean you are unintelligent, but I do mean you are probably unaware—very much in the dark.

There is a corollary state to the condition of lack of awareness: it is being *unconsciously competent*—it is doing things in concert with universal law—without knowing it. Take the seagull's ability to open clamshells, for example. It is a dangerous state to be in because it leads to complacency and satisfaction. In life, you either are creating or disintegrating. Complacency and satisfaction are the beginning of a disintegrating state. Instead, you should consider adopting an attitude of inspirational dissatisfaction.

We had discovered in our practice a strategy that worked for us—but we were completely unaware of the dynamics behind the strategy. There was a hiccup in the flow of our operation (when one of the partners panicked and quit) and what we thought was going to be a lifetime relationship disappeared before our eyes as his relationship with us died.

The laws of the universe came to our aid in a very simple way. Instead of looking for the disastrous elements of what *had* happened, we purposefully decided to look for the good—the seeds of a greater benefit in the midst of the disaster: the can-do part of the situation.

Immediately, we withdrew our energy from the act of standing around stunned about the disaster that had befallen our firm. Then we consciously focused it on the decision-making process of deciding *what to do to survive* and thrive. We attracted those opportunities. We made a purposeful decision to thrive and survive. We did not know how—and we now know we did not *have* to know, because we had the faith and expectation that we would achieve what we believed.

As is always the case, the way was shown—simply by our paying attention—like being on a heightened state of alert—and we are prepared for the opportunities and possibilities our thoughts could attract.

We acted on the plan that would give us the opportunity not only to survive but to thrive and to succeed exponentially. All of this happened through the power of thought and belief despite being in the state of not knowing how! We did not have to know how.

We had escaped the prison of unawareness simply by being aware of how the universal laws work.

An Idea That Seemed to Come Out of Nowhere But Made Me $300,000

It never fails to amaze me how so often the minutest inkling of an idea can turn into a huge bonanza. We were in the midst of doing document discovery in a group of asbestos cases. The records of the defendant—an asbestos manufacturer—were in a practically abandoned industrial building in the Hell's Kitchen section of New York City.

The defendant kept stalling on giving us access to the documents until an unbearable heat wave struck the city in the middle of August. Of course, there was no air conditioning, virtually no air circulation, and the temperature on the top floor of this building was 103 degrees.

We were in the company of a young associate of the defense firm who was there to keep his eye on us. We all trudged up to the fifth floor—the top floor of this elevatorless building—and were confronted with what seemed like an airplane hangar sized room with thousands of filing cabinets—most of them rusting and pretty seriously banged up. Even opening the drawers was going to be a challenge.

I was wondering if we had wasted our time even trying to find any incriminating documents. We knew we were facing thirty or forty years of personnel records pertaining to our disabled clients. And man was it hot and sticky. The heat was so bad it was actually dangerous. Hell's Kitchen, all right.

For two days, we scrounged through filing cabinet after filing cabinet. We had to take a break on the first day, find a nearby hardware store, and invest in a giant crowbar to help us get into some of the dented filing cabinets. Every molecule of our bodies was screaming for us to give up. Moreover, surveying the huge room of cabinets was more than discouraging. How were we ever going to find any of the files we needed—especially since we suspected the company had destroyed them a long time ago?

This was definitely a situation in which giving up could be rationalized!

Nevertheless, when I felt like quitting, Jay urged me on; and when Jay insisted we give up, I encouraged him to hang in there.

That, my friend, is when we struck gold.

We found hitherto undisclosed correspondence between various thermal insulation manufacturers that acknowledged a connection between asbestos exposure and cancer. It was the beginning of a conspiracy of silence—and Jay and I had found hard, incontrovertible evidence of it. Actually, what we had found was a thousand times more valuable than gold. The defendant probably had no idea the evidence even existed.

However, how were we to get all of this stuff out of there? We faced a defensive guard dog who would report to his superiors what we had found—and we urgently needed to maintain the element of surprise. On top of that obstacle, there was the sweltering heat, no elevator, and no photocopier.

Then I had an idea.

Jay and I went out and found a portable air conditioner. We lugged it back up to the fifth floor. We set it up in a small office off the main storage room. We told the guard dog that we needed to air condition the small space and that we'd bring the files from the main room (it would be pointless to try to lower the temperature in such a huge space, we pointed out) and review them in the now air conditioned office.

We turned the A.C. on and decided to adjourn for lunch. And here was the brilliant part. The guard dog was a drinker, and Jay and I began to challenge each other to drinking shot after shot and, without us egging the guard dog on in any way, he chose to try to pace us.

Now, whether or not I had signaled the waiter to pour two of us highly diluted scotch, I cannot recall; but I am pretty sure the guard dog's drinks were full strength.

Suffice it to say, when we get back to the air-conditioned room, the guard dog gets comfortable and sleepy. We maneuver some boxes to improvise ottomans for the three rickety chairs we have, and all three of us put our feet up and seem to kind of doze off. Once the guard dog is in a deep sleep, Jay and I jump up, dash down the block to an office supply store and immediately convince the manager to rent us a photocopier. It was well worth whatever outrageous fee we paid for it, believe me. The guard dog dozed while we photocopied to our heart's content.

Fast-forward several months to our perfectly timed revelation to the asbestos industry that we had the smoking guns. The manufacturers were in big trouble. The conspiracy of silence quickly crumbled. Furthermore, we would earn a fortune in settlement fees over the next few years.

How did all of this happen? It started with a little idea about creature comfort and our knowledge that most people would rather be comfortable than diligent.

Is it all true? Most of it, save for a little poetic license. One thing for sure, our discovery was the beginning of the end to an industry's conspiracy about the health effects of exposure to asbestos!

In Your Brain's Eye?

99% of the lawyers practicing in the United States believe that 99% of their knowledge comes from their brains. Furthermore, most of them are in the group of 80% of attorneys who—together—scramble to earn 20% of the money made in our profession.

If I could get them all in one room, the first thing I'd tell them is that the number one reason they are "on stuck" in their professional careers is that they are confusing their brains with their minds—and the same probably goes for their personal lives.

Your brain is a tiny, tiny, tiny subset of your mind. It is what a lug nut is to a car; an essential part, but far from the sum total.

Knowledge is a thing—a noun—that is generated from the act of knowing—a verb. Knowledge consists of ideas, thoughts, facts, experiences and emotions that exist in the universe into which we, as thinking beings, have the privilege of tapping into—any time we choose.

You *know* with your physical senses that you saw a flying saucer. However, appearances can be deceiving.

You have ideas, thoughts, observations, facts, experiences, and emotions running through your mind.

Actually, you know *about* flying saucers, you have thoughts about them, you certainly saw some lights in the sky, and you felt fear and exhilaration.

You *know* you saw a flying saucer.

That is what you know.

Here is what *I* know.

I know that last night around 9 p.m., the Air Force meteorologists at nearby Willow Grove Naval Air Station were practicing altitude maneuvers with illuminated night weather balloons.

You saw a flying saucer and I saw the 11 o'clock news. In addition, I guarantee you somebody else saw something else.

So much for knowledge and the brain's ability to process ideas, thoughts, facts, experiences, and emotions.

Knowing takes place at a higher level of awareness.

You may play golf and think you know the game. Yet, may I suggest that a golf professional, especially one who has been well coached, "knows" the game at a different level.

As lawyers, we may be well educated, but most of us have not been well coached—if we had been coached at all.

We know the game of lawyering. Nevertheless, at what level do we know it? How well do we *really* know it?

SUCCESS
FROM THE INSIDE OUT

The superior man is the providence of the inferior.
He is eyes for the blind, strength for the weak, and
a shield for the defenseless.
He stands erect by bending above the fallen.
He rises by lifting others.

—Robert Green Ingersoll

Are You Moving Around, Or Actually Doing Something?

"Never confuse motion with action."
—Ernest Hemingway

Did you ever have one of those days when you work from dawn to dusk and then wonder where all those hours went—because you sure did not accomplish anything?

You were working from the outside in.

I am 99% certain I can solve your problem in about twenty seconds:

You simply failed to plan how to handle all the interruptions. That is inside out. Germinate the solution from the inside to handle the activity from the outside.

If you had said something like, "I'll talk to everyone who calls—but I won't call anyone back until after 3 o'clock"—or, "until I finish this brief, I'm not moving a muscle, even if the building is burning"—your productivity would have been very different.

On those seemingly unproductive days, you probably had a great plan of attack *for what you wanted to accomplish*—but you simply left the backdoor unlocked, and half the neighborhood wandered in.

Lock the door and get 50% more work accomplished every day.

By the way, developing a workable method to man-age the inevitable interruptions should be a part of *every day* you go to work.

Napoleon Hill's Ideas On Positive Attitude

Attorneys who struggle in their practices naturally become quite familiar with—*too* familiar with—negative thinking.

However, since we so deeply imbed negative thinking into our being, it may not be apparent that we can replace it with something so highly effective.

Napoleon Hill bases much of his work on the concept that you can absolutely replace your old attitude with a positive mental attitude.

Hill believes that a Positive Mental Attitude is the single most important principle of the science of success, without which you cannot get the maximum benefit from the other sixteen principles.

Success attracts success and failure attracts more failure.

Your mental attitude is the only thing over which you, and only you, have complete control.

A Positive Mental Attitude attracts opportunities for success, while a Negative Mental Attitude repels opportunities and does not even take advantage of them when they do come along.

A positive mind finds a way to do it... a negative mind looks for all the ways it cannot.

Hill is plain in his language referring to two major universal laws: the law of attraction and the law of vibration. They are sisters. You attract to your world that with which you are in harmony.

For example, think back to the last time when you had to force yourself to do something—something positive.

What was it?

Was it getting started on a project?

Was it getting out of bed when you did not feel like it?

Maybe it was pushing you away from some unhealthy or unnecessary food.

All those are examples of using Positive Mental Attitude to get you to do something. However, they are also examples of *unconscious* Positive Mental Attitude. When you do it consciously—wow!—you become unstoppable. And the beauty of it is—*you can learn to develop that skill, just as simply as you can learn a new computer software program.*

Imagine if you could summon up that kind of energy *all the time—whenever you felt like it.* Imagine how powerful you would become.

Believing Something Is Different Than Knowing Something

There are only two places that you can go if you seriously study these ideas about making your changes from the inside out.

One is science and the other is theology.

In the 21st century, more people are comfortable with science and suspicious of theology. There is an important reason for this: you can see, feel, smell, hear, and in other ways quantify things in the scientific realm. Theology, on the other hand, requires an entire array of senses that have atrophied in most of us.

You can rejuvenate your senses, but it will take some genuine motivation to revisit those dormant—or even worse, *purposefully ignored*—senses. Call it intentional negligence.

I have looked at each, for both personal reasons as well as for my law practice, and gone to the extreme in each one.

In the 17th century, science and theology split. They used to be sister studies. However, the people of power wanted more power and they said, "My way is the only way and your way is wrong."

Therefore, science went one direction and theology went the other.

Now, what is belief? I wanted to know which discipline it was.

"Belief is to accept as true or real."

To accept as true or real. That is what it says in the dictionary.

What do you accept as true or real?

Acceptance is a choice. The only real power you have in this world is choice. What are you going to accept as a belief for yourself about any subject? Then ask yourself why. "Why am I going to believe these things?"

You believe them because someone else told you it is the truth, so a lot people (your culture, the media, your religion, your professional association, for example) convinced you it was true.

Now, if from the perspective of a practicing attorney, you really look at this word "belief," you will see that it really is very powerful. Throughout your practice, it is your beliefs that guide your actions. However, beliefs are different from knowledge, and, believe me, it is easy to forget that there is a difference.

I know a person who won an absolute immunity action against an attorney who defamed him, despite the "absolute" part of the immunity. How did he do this? Because he realized that most lawyers and judges naturally believed that "absolute" meant *absolute*—but of course, in law as in life, *nothing* is absolute, despite a label that might call it that. This *pro se* researched the law when other lawyers concluded the case was unwinnable.

They were wrong. They held a belief and made the mistake of thinking it was knowledge.

The litigant did not have to share his damages award with any one of us.

We've Forgotten How to be Lawyers

We have forgotten how to think creatively.

It's that simple.

We are in stimulus-react mode.

Because of the competitive nature of our business today, we react, we do not act—and we have become so lost that we accept reflexive reaction and call it thinking,

If we are not careful, we will wind up like the doctors: a commodity sitting on the shelf, waiting for the lowest bidder to come in on Dollar Discount Day.

You can change it, but first, you have to be reacquainted with your identity—or better yet, you have to know you have lost it.

Remember, It's an Inside Job

Because we attorneys seek out legal precedents to support our clients' positions, we sometimes have to rely on precedents that are either not exactly on the mark (when there are no cases on point), or sometimes even really stretchhhhhhhhh a precedent and just pray it will hold up.

That kind of thinking sometimes works in the law, but it is not really a sound way to become more and more successful. Moreover, it reminds me of something Napoleon Hill said: "There is a difference between wishing for a thing and being ready to receive it. No one is ready for a thing until he believes he can acquire it. The state of mind must be belief, not mere hope or wish. Open-mindedness is essential for belief. Closed minds do not inspire faith, courage, and belief."

You have to be willing to learn. You have to be willing to say that there is a condition in your life and you do not really care for it.

Then you have to discover *how* it came to be in your life, and then you have to figure out exactly how you are going to get it out of your life and how you are going to replace it with something vastly better.

Until you do that, you are trying to change from the outside in, and that just does not create anything permanent.

Never has.

Never will.

It's physically impossible because the real you will eventually re-emerge, thinking the same thoughts and taking the same actions and—presto!—the same result.

You may make changes but, as Emerson once said, "Of what value to make heroic vows of amendment, when it is the same old law breaker trying to keep them?"

First, you must change.

Stranger In the Mirror

Lawyers have become human cookie cutters.

It's no wonder young attorneys today have trouble earning $45,000 annually.

Cookie cutters are commodity products—and what happened to computers, and what is happening to the medical profession, is happening to us.

India-based law firms are selling top-notch legal research for $25 an hour over the Internet!

Moreover, unless each lawyer who wants to succeed actively does something about it, we will be like the complete computer systems you can now buy for $499.

There is practically no margin in those systems. The computer stores pray you will buy software and inkjet cartridges—because that is the only place there is still any profit in retail tech.

That is what is happening to *us*.

Fee income will drop, costs will remain fixed or rise, and we will be $499 computers sitting on shelves as loss leaders.

We follow the crowd, we just try to do what the other guy does and the result is just more of the same.

It is killing the profession.

Just like that fly that keeps flying into the window screen trying to get to the bowl of fruit. He does not even *think* about finding another way in—like the open door five feet to the left. He is programmed to make a beeline for the fruit bowl, just to keep trying until he succeeds or dies. His strategy is simply to *try harder!* In this case—and in many other situations including, possibly, *your situation*—trying harder is a fatal mistake.

That is ignorance—not stupidity—just literally ignorance.

We keep repeating the same mistakes we have been making, hoping for a different result.

Nevertheless, things keep getting worse.

If we have no sense of identity, anything can happen to us, and we probably will not even know it.

SUCCESS
FROM THE INSIDE OUT

Yes, there is such a thing as luck in trial law but it only comes at 3 o'clock in the morning. You'll still find me in the library looking for luck at 3 o'clock in the morning.

—Louis Nizer

Balance

What you are really looking for is a balanced life. Most people—and especially most lawyers who are so caught up in their day-to-day stress and deadlines—do not even realize it. No one would trade a huge balance in his or her checking account for genuine joy and happiness, just as no one would trade being broke and frustrated for being a millionaire dying of cancer. Most people believe they need money. They do not. They need what they think the money will help them get. Amazingly, our species has gotten this far with that kind of thinking!

INSIDE OUT INSIGHT: People really do not often think past the next move.
To reach a happy state of existence, you should be doing what you love and have enough money to live the way you want to live. This is a balanced life. Most lawyers do not believe they can do this. They just do not. Instead, they talk about big cases, files that got away from them, unfair judges. They tell you many things, but very few of them are on point.

You will be amazed at how much free time you have when you never have to think about money. If you understand the laws of success as well as you understand the laws of the state you practice in, you will not ever have to worry about money. Once you learn the laws, once you *understand* the laws, you do not have to worry about money.

Where Have All the Great Lawyers Gone?

The great lawyers of yesterday were willing to accept responsibility for the coming generations.

Today's attorneys just keep turning in this year's Jag for next years.

The big boys today get caught up in the wave of greed and competition—which I acknowledge is damned powerful—and their pride does not allow them to embrace the classic success technologies that had been passed on to them by their mentors.

Listen, when the attorney general of the United States goes to jail—and when a president (who is an attorney!) in 1972 gets indicted—you can understand how that sent us on a tailspin and we didn't began to recover until we elected a preachery kind of country lawyer.

However, that did not last too long. Next thing you know we have another lawyer in the White House who is using the Oval Office for the same reason friends used to ask you if they could use a spare bedroom when your parents were out for the night.

It was not a real image booster for the profession.

SUCCESS
FROM THE INSIDE OUT

Three from one of the greatest attorneys of all time—Clarence Darrow:

I have suffered from being misunderstood, but I would have suffered a hell of a lot more if I had been understood.

If you lose the power to laugh, you lose the power to think.

When I was a boy, I was told that anybody could become President; I'm beginning to believe it.

Size Matters?

The numbers generated by our practices, the extent of our possessions, the hourly rates we can get away with and size of our staff have infatuated our minds.

The ridiculous truth is we have become obsessed with the size of our staff.

"I hope if dogs ever take over the world, and they chose a king, they don't just go by size, because I bet there are some Chihuahuas out there with some really good ideas."
—Jack Handy

Time Out: To Remind Yourself of Who You Are

"Each of us literally chooses, by his way of attending to things, what sort of universe he shall appear to himself to inhabit."
—William James

Do you really know who you are?

Are you who other people think you are?

If not, do you want to be who other people think you are?

Knowing who you are and/or who you want to be is THE starting point for all success.

If You Can't Wait to Get to the Office In the Morning...

...why not?

Keep reading and stick with the ideas in *Power of Attorney*, and you will—absolutely—wake up refreshed and chomping on the bit to get to the office. There will not be any other place in the world that is more fun.

The "G" Word

You know, I work with lawyers, politicians, cops, doctors, judges and everyone else all day long.

You can usually bring the foul language you hear virtually everywhere to a dead stop—just like that!—by using the "g" word—by that, of course, I mean the "God" word.

People put up with so much colorful language that they tune out almost everything, but—wow!—when you throw the "g" word in there, watch out. You will get reactions across the spectrum of possibilities. From reverence, to abuse, to being laughed at in your face, and the worst, the looks of belittlement, like, "What's that poor sap bringing God into this for?"

You should see the battles rage between the believers and non-believers about capitalization.

"How dare you not capitalize God?"

"How dare you actually print the word? It must be respected and printed like this: G-d."

"How dare you capitalize a fairy tale character and then bow down to it?"

Oh, come on man.

It's an idea.

Take it easy.

Relax.

Well, what you believe about God—if anything—

is completely, 100% your business.

However, why your beliefs are important in *Power of Attorney* is that in order to succeed with the ideas presented here, you need to believe in something—some power, some *consciousness*—greater than your self. That can include a power (for lack of a better word) that is deep within your deeper self that you have never fully accessed.

If you do not believe in *some* kind of superior consciousness, then that means you believe you are at the top of the food chain in terms of consciousness, and that is where we—you and I—become directly at odds.

I DO believe in something—though I won't define it here because what I personally believe in isn't relevant, just that I do believe in something, that it exists, and that by understanding, I become more powerful, purposeful and determined to succeed. Because, in part, it becomes clearer to me that I absolutely can, without a single doubt, succeed beyond my wildest dreams.

Are you with me or agin' me?

Please Don't Tell My Mother I'm a Lawyer...

I don't want to disappoint her

...She thinks I'm the nighttime piano player at the local bordello.

I am pretty certain that's a new low.

Who's Having More Fun Practicing the Law Than Me?

If the answer isn't "Me!" then you're working too hard.

In addition, if you *are* having more fun than I am, I want to talk to you.

Death of a Lawyer

Take a break from this book and go out and rent *Death of a Salesman*—the original with Lee J. Cobb, or the new one with Dustin Hoffman.

Your call.

But the idea is the same.

We attorneys are salesmen of abstract ideas, and there are masters of selling out there whom we've ignored from time immemorial who can help us. We need to use them, avail ourselves of their expertise; otherwise, we will keep on heading in the same direction.

Moreover, what happens to Willie Loman in *Death of a Salesman* is an object lesson on what can and does happen to attorneys. Not in the precisely same way, but you will get the idea.

Brainstorms

When it comes to solving problems—at home or in your law practice—your subconscious mind loves the task and works at finding solutions 24 hours a day.

All the same, when the solutions come, they may not be instantly recognizable. For me, they often come as brainstorms that seem to have nothing to do with the problem. I know that over the years, I have lost many great ideas because I failed to spend fifteen seconds writing down the gist of the thought. Only after it is too late, or in the midst of oral arguments, or in the courtroom, do I recall that, yes, I once did know the answer to that! But I failed to appreciate the gift and I let it sail away.

Moreover, if you do not carry a pen and a piece of paper or a digital device to help you, you are going to be in trouble when it comes to remembering your brainstorms.

This is especially important for lawyers who are trying to think their clients out of bad legal positions.

"When you get a brainstorm, lock it up," my friend, Sid Friedman, once told me. I recently interviewed him about the kinds of thoughts that hit you like an anvil —the kinds of thoughts that you just know are higher quality than your average daydream.

"You have to capture your brainstorms," Sid says, "because they are gifts from nature, and they will evaporate as a dream does if you don't document them. The most important thing to remember about a brainstorm is to write everything down immediately. Do not trust your memory. Your brain may work like a computer, but the recall is only as good as the way you store the data."

Inside Out Insight: They are gifts of nature, yes, but scientifically explainable. When you relax and allow your subconscious to search the universe in its effort to attract the answer, it will locate it. Resonate with it, attract it, and bingo! You have it. It has done the job. Now you must write it down. It was in this way that Edison discovered the elusive material that finally worked as the filament for the incandescent light bulb.

These days, if you pop into Radio Shack you can pick up a digital voice recorder for under a hundred bucks and download your thoughts into your computer to see them instantly on the screen or on paper.

Ideas are like dreams. They will absolutely fade away as the day's distractions intensify. Write them down, and they are yours to own forever, let them fade away and you may never know what you have missed.

Be More Than Just Someone's Lawyer

Do things most lawyers do not even think of doing —at least most of the 80% of all lawyers who never get anywhere.

Try these things to achieve an instant positive, upbeat reaction from your clients today—and a measurable increase in business in the future.

- Call to follow up on a file—without the client calling first. Create an actual schedule to do this.
- Create a brief "client bio" that lists things of interest to your client, then hire a high school or college kid to spend a few hours a week combing through newspapers and periodicals for the sole purpose of finding things that may be of interest to this person. Send a clipping to the client via the postal service (pay for the stamp, do not use email) and let the client know that you are thinking of him or her.
- Send your clients abstracts of cases relevant to their files—even if they aren't legally literate—it still shows you are interested in them.
- Ask clients what the most important day of the year is to them—make a note and send them a card on the appropriate date.

While you are doing this stuff, do not forget to *listen*. If you do not listen, then all of the above is invalid. Treat the client as if you were the client.

Why do this?

It is the Golden Rule—Do unto Others as You Would Have Others Do unto You.

It is another way of restating the Law of Cause and Effect. For every action, there is an equal and opposite reaction. Therefore, whatever you put out there does come back equally. It is as if you yourself are the others.

Apply the Law of Cause and Effect and you create your own destiny.

More On Attitude

That your attitude is everything is a cliché—but for a good reason.

What do I mean?

Your attitude is the composite of your thoughts, feelings, and actions. There is nothing else to you than this. We live in a thought universe, inside a thought world and exist simultaneously on three parallel planes.

The importance of realizing that there are three simultaneous levels of existence comes into play when you want to change your results. The best way to change your results is by working from the inside out.

INSIDE OUT INSIGHT: It is an inside job.

It is your attitude; how you see yourself—your self-image, your paradigm or your conditioning—the label is irrelevant. It is what determines what you get in life. It acts as an autopilot. It is so automatic; you do not even realize you have it, like your heartbeat.

However, once you do begin to consider the nature of attitude, you step up your level of awareness. It is part of the jailbreak from the prison of ignorance.

This is exactly what happened to my partners and me.

While we knew we had a good thing in our Three

Musketeer relationship, we only viewed it from that classical sense of all for one and one for all—without knowing exactly the potency of its psychological influence.

SUCCESS
FROM THE INSIDE OUT

Self-respect is the fruit of discipline; the sense of dignity grows with the ability to say no to oneself.

—Abraham J. Heschel

Mastermind Alliances

What is a mastermind alliance?

As Napoleon Hill states, "The Master Mind may be defined as: coordination of knowledge and effort, in a spirit of harmony, between two or more people, for the attainment of a definite purpose."

Very few successful people do it by themselves. In fact, I say "very few" out of a sense of fair play, because the truth is that I know of no one who has done it on his or her own. There are many who *think* they have; in fact, they probably did not.

Make a point of finding other attorneys who believe in succeeding from the inside out and form an informal coalition to help each other, bat around ideas, and give each other encouragement. Do this with extreme care.

The road you are on is not an easy one. The rewards are great, but the work is hard.

Part Three

SELLING IT TO THE JUDGE AND JURY

You are the judge and jury of your own life. If you make convincing arguments built on solid precedent, you are guaranteed to win—in court, but not in life.

In life, you must have a goal and an understanding, faith and expectation in a desired outcome. You must accept the responsibility to execute the plans that materialize—and you can never, ever give up.

Letting the Inmates Run the Asylum

Over the years, the information you accept into your mind accumulates into habits as it enters into the subconscious (feelings) portions of your mind.

That part of your mind has no power to accept or reject.

Some people confuse the subconscious with the *unconscious*. That is a big mistake.

Not only are they not the same, they are vastly different animals: the subconscious is a violently powerful state. The unconscious is simply a passive state.

So what happens in our minds over time?

We form habits. We become a certain way through conditioning—we create a personality without realizing it, and we develop a habitual way of being and thinking. We are actually living someone else's life.

We tend to ignore the idea of *being*.

Man is a *human becoming*.

I propose you take a close look at that term. We are physical and spiritual entities, guided by our physical senses.

The "physical" part of the term is that we are "human"—and the spiritual part of the term is the word "being." The spiritual or (non-physical) part is most of what we are, only we do not know it or are not aware of it. We tend to forget about it and come to see ourselves solely as physical entities.

And it's easy to do that because unless we are consciously aware of our minds all or most of the time, we are getting most of our information from our five senses—which are, of course, all physical.

Now, about the brain, that is a physical thing. You think with it. It is an electrical center that puts you into action, but that is it.

The mind, however, is a spiritual thing. Of course, the brain informs the mind, but the mind still exists without it. It is non-physical. The law of opposites dictates this must be true. If there is an up, there must be a down. If there is a physical, there must be a non-physical.

It is our feelings that propel us into action.

Imagine that if you had no experience or knowledge of a black widow spider, you might just sit still on your picnic blanket while one crawled over to you. But your actual knowledge—having seen a documentary about black widows—as well as your *emotional reaction* to them is what propels you into action—in this case, either wild stomping or getting up and leaving.

Since it is the feeling portion of our minds that stimulates us to action, it tends to act robotically, or as Dr. Maxwell Maltz described, as a *cybernetic mechanism* (also known as an autopilot). We are not aware that we can control the mechanism that keeps us imprisoned in unawareness. Given authority by the misconception that "that's just the way it is," or "it isn't my destiny," or "I don't have the right upbringing," et cetera.

None of these conditions is the truth, but they just appear that way in the subconscious mind, so your self-image causes you to take actions habitually consistent with that image. You act in life to follow the model established in your subconscious mind.

Moreover, this is preposterously unfair, because you had little or no input into your subconscious. You never had the opportunity to accept or reject the elements of it.

Until now!

Now you have to study this stuff, see what makes sense to you—do not take my word for it. It is too important to leave to a stranger!

You are conditioned to act in whatever way your subconscious is programmed, without much control. However, once the mechanism is revealed (that is what is happening right this second) and becomes apparent to you, you can make it work to your advantage instead of what most likely has been happening to you your entire life.

When you let your subconscious mind direct your life—without you having very much of a clue about what programs it's running—you are doing nothing less than letting the inmates run the asylum. It may make an interesting movie script, but it is a hell of a way to run your life.

This book is about change.

Understanding precedes change; it is not a result of it.

However, change you must if you want your results to change.

Eye On the Ball

In one of his great film roles, Kevin Costner plays a major league pitcher who seems to be at the end of his career. In the film *For Love of the Game*, he gives us a hint about how to control the mechanism about which we have been talking. Have you ever wondered how a professional athlete can perform under pressure, repeatedly, consistently?

When Costner is about to deliver the pitch, the surrounding crowd noise is deafening, he has little room for error, and the batter is out for blood.

Yet Costner delivers the pitch at just the right velocity at just the right spot, and strikes out "Mighty Casey."

How does he do it?

If you watch the film closely, you will hear him say, "mechanism on" and he changes his mental state, shutting out all surrounding distractions, and his body knows how to do the rest. He has discovered the principle *and he has practiced it*. He is in control of his cybernetic mechanism—his autopilot.

Therefore, while most people thought the movie was about a heroic but washed up major league pitcher, I see it as a film about the power of the subconscious mind —should you choose to control it.

The term *practicing law from the inside out* means

that you are in control of your conditioned mind, subconscious mind, and self-image: they are all part of the same.

It means you are exercising the miraculous power you have as a human being.

It means the power no other species has: the power of choice.

Again, at first, we were unconsciously exerting this power and ignorant of the ramifications and results we could create with the conscious exercise of this power.

We were unaware of a law just as absolute as the law of gravity and that worked in exactly the same way. They call it the law of attraction. A universal law allowing you to attract to yourself whatever energy—physical or non-physical—with which you are in harmony, i.e., clients. That's right, attracting clients.

When we as a law firm were in harmony with positive, profitable things and people, you would be surprised what showed up on our law firm's plate.

You don't believe it?

See what happens.

When we vibrated disharmoniously—by not having a mutual purpose, by thinking about 'what's in it for me' instead of thinking "for the firm"—disaster showed up.

Naturally, we attributed the events to accident, fate, or plain old bad luck.

Only now, in retrospect, do we clearly see what and who was responsible—us, and the kinds of things we thought about—and, significantly, *failed to think about*.

When we did realize we had so much more control, we began to manage it.

Moreover, today we have gross sales of more than $20 million annually.

Our success is a *direct result* of becoming aware of how we, as human beings, think.

SUCCESS
FROM THE INSIDE OUT

I know of no higher fortitude than stubbornness in the face of overwhelming odds.

—Louis Nizer

"Infinite Potential?"

"Infinite Potential"
I use that term a lot.
Many people roll their eyes.
Infinite potential.
Don't buy it?
Then what do *you* call it?

Learning to be a prosperous attorney from the inside out is all about teaching you how to get in sync with that infinite potential.

Learning how to do this is not really a strategy or set of techniques: it is an attitude. It is an attitude of life.

I want you to ask yourself what you really want. What do you *really* want? Many times, we think this means excluding something from our lives. Well, I can have this, but if I have this, I cannot have that. I think we do that because we believe that there's a lack of abundance out there. Intellectually, we know that there is abundance, but I do not think we believe it, because we make decisions that say there is not abundance. If you believed it, you would not make those decisions. What do you really want? Do you remember what we said about infinite potential? You have infinite potential, and we say, "I know." So what do you really want? You have to think here. What do you really want? "I don't know." That pattern is going to cause great problems for you if you do not break through it. There is a saying, "Know the truth and the truth will set you free."

It will set you free from what?

INSIDE OUT INSIGHT: You need to be free from only one thing and that is ignorance. Ignorance keeps you in a place where "you don't know." There's no faith there; there's no studying there; there's no acting out on things, because you feel if you do, you're going to lose in some way, instead of believing there is an abundance in your life. There truly is abundance. With knowledge, you are free. With ignorance, you are in prison. I do not know of anyone who ever breaks completely free of this prison. They really don't. Because they do not know things and they do not even know that they don't know.

Most people are walking around in a fog and do not even know where to turn for answers. The smart thing to do is find someone who does know. Most people will not. They will say, "I better go back and just deal with reality and go back to work." They go right back into a comfort zone.

You do not know that you do not know. We all have these things inside of us. The truth is that you *do* know. You just have to know where to look. Animals are born with instinct. An animal knows after birth to go to the breast for nourishment. However, the animal does not know that it knows that. It is just an instinct. You do not have to teach a baby how to suck, and that is a complicated thing. You just put the baby to the breast. You might have to show the baby how to get the nipple in his mouth, but when he does, he instinctively knows how to suck.

Nevertheless, we go through our lives and do not seem to have any direction. The truth is, you do have direction, but you do not see it. That direction is inside every one of us now, but only if you believe in a Higher Power. You have to know that God, or Infinite Intelligence, would not put you here without some kind of direction. Even an oak tree has a direction; it is growing up. Everything is for greater growth. Everything is for more abundance.

What we do not have is an awareness of what that is. We need to start to thinking about that awareness. We have to think about becoming more aware of who we are and what we are capable of doing. Because all you are really going to do in this life is raise your level of awareness, and you are going to do it one step at a time. The truth is, you do know.

Brainstorms, Part II

Here is an idea to help you stimulate brainstorms to solve tricky legal or business problems:

Sit down, take out a note pad or a voice recorder, and start to think while you jot down or say key words and phrases ("find a cause of action," "how can I improve the contract's terms," or "advertising ideas for more clients.") Then, quiet your mind and listen to that still, small voice inside for the inspired answers. When they come, write them down without judgment. Let it flow.

This exercise can actually precipitate brainstorms, which can come immediately—or maybe not for days or weeks.

Nevertheless, by sitting down and trying, you are baiting a hook in your mind, and eventually the right idea will swim by and take a bite.

You are now "thinking" with your higher mental faculties.

I am sure you are familiar with the phenomenon of learning a new word—a word that you cannot recall ever having seen or heard before. Then, within 24 hours, you have somehow seen, read, or heard that exact word used half a dozen times!

Well, when you create "cells of recognition" in your mind by thinking about what you want to find, you will increase your ability to find it. It is not because of magic, but because of one of the Laws of Success.

SUCCESS
FROM THE INSIDE OUT

Destiny is not a matter of chance, it is a matter of choice; it is not a thing to be waited for, it is a thing to be achieved.

—William Jennings Bryan

Marketing for Lawyers, Part I

Years ago when, as a young lawyer, you left law school, perhaps did your apprenticeship and landed your first real job, you were told that all you needed to do in order to be successful financially was to be a good lawyer and the word will get around. You will have more clients than you know what to do with.

While that was all right for the middle part of the twentieth century, it is no longer a key to success in the "business" of the practice of law.

There has been a fundamental increase in the number of lawyers and there is unbelievable competition for the legal work that is out there. Most importantly, there is the realization by the larger firms that every piece of business is potentially something they should be handling.

Thus the perception that the legal services pie is shrinking. In this section, we will deal with the legal application of the five fundamentals of marketing. I have successfully applied these mindsets and strategies and have seen them used in law firms of varying sizes from the sole practitioner to the mega firms.

However, the first hurdle you must overcome is the idea that you need not market your services and that just hanging out your shingle and telling a few friends is all you need in the business of practicing law to achieve your financial goals. It is clearly a combination of marketing principles, strategies, and most important, attitude that are needed. In fact, if you have to choose only one thing from that list, it would have to be attitude—a *certain* attitude.

Marketing for Lawyers, Part II

The problem with marketing is that most of us would rather not do it. We do not know what it really is, anyway; and most of it does not work.

We are so "wrapped up" in our practice; it is so time consuming; there are so many pressures; and for most of us, the lawyering aspects are so all-consuming that we tend to ignore the marketing side of our business.

We will read an article, attend a seminar, have a discussion with a colleague, get excited, make a "heroic vow of amendment" but we remain the "same old" when it comes to marketing.

As I said, most marketing does not work. Therefore, the real marketing geniuses out there are the ones who have seen many more failures than successes, but once they do find something that succeeds they work off of it.

There are fundamental, essential marketing building blocks that will allow you to get control of the little things that really make your practice grow exponentially.

Such little things include new client acquisitions, retention of old clients, maximizing referrals from many different sources, and attracting only "perfect clients." "Perfect clients" are those whom you enjoy representing; in fact, when you think about it, why should you represent anyone else?

The idea of birds of a feather in terms of the lawyer-client relationship is not new and does not mean that some clients, which could be profit centers for the firm, go elsewhere. It just means that you have to find someone of like mind and attitude to handle clients who are not congruent with your personality. Just the recognition that you have a choice in this matter and then acting on that recognition can do wonders.

Jay Abraham, who many believe is a true "marketing genius" and the foremost authority on growing the entrepreneurial model business, said that there are only three ways to grow your business. You can increase the number of clients; you can increase the number of times you sell something to the client; or you can increase the average sale to each client. These are fundamentals of growing a service business and it just necessitates some "out of the box" thinking in order to apply these fundamental principles to the practice of law.

INSIDE OUT INSIGHT: Do not say at this point that you cannot do that, because I have to tell you that law firms all over the country already are doing it, and are seeing exponential growth by just realizing and understanding these fundamental principles.

By asking yourself how you can do these three things, you will begin the thinking process. This is a creative thinking process so you should do it in a quiet place where you will not be disturbed. You should begin by writing down the following: how can I increase the number of my clients; the frequency with which I serve these clients; increase the average sale to each client. Just do this exercise and see what comes out.

You will be amazed.

What happens if you are stuck? What happens if you just do not know?

Keep your mind working by asking, out loud if necessary, "if I *did* know" how would I...?

Inside out success technologies are easy to understand *intellectually*, but quite challenging at times to execute.

It is supposed to be that way, so if that is what you are experiencing, then take comfort in that you are on the right track.

Marketing for Lawyers, Part III

As an evening student at Temple University in the late 60s and early 70s, a rather eccentric professor told me that we, as lawyers, were nothing but "hucksters of abstract ideas."

I recently confirmed this notion through a conversation with a well-known trial lawyer who, as he traveled throughout the state and country trying cases, viewed himself as a "traveling salesman."

Now some of you may be saying to yourselves that referring to us as salespeople is somewhat demeaning.

Nothing could be further from the truth. The highest paid professionals in the world are salespeople. In fact, if you look at it objectively, most of us are paid a draw against our annual salary every year. Then at year-end, whether we are working for a large firm or for ourselves, a bonus is paid in the form of a percentage commission, based upon the level of success we have achieved in generating revenue for the entity. Sales training and sales psychology is fundamental in being happy and successful as a lawyer.

We have just resisted the training seminars and preaching that have long been out there, which some of the more open-minded of us have adopted.

Clients stay with you, or come to you, for only one reason: they are experiencing some kind of an affinity. Something you have said or done in their presence or by reputation has "attracted" them; thus, even perhaps unconsciously you have taken advantage of the "law of attraction" which is one of the fundamental universal laws behind any marketing plan.

Regardless of what pathway you choose and what marketing technique a law firm marketing specialist recommends to you there is one outstanding fundamental that, far above all the rest, will dictate your success or failure from a marketing standpoint. That fundamental is the "relationship" that you create between your client, the firm, and all the firms' sub-parts.

Simply stated, if clients like dealing with you, they will deal with you more often, spend more money, and they will recommend other similarly feathered clients to you.

It is a simple idea, but it is not easy to implement because it involves change, and understanding the dynamics of relationships—subjects that lawyers are steadfastly resistant to accepting. Sure, there are individuals and business out there that will, in the short run, undertake your services for a limited purpose, but they are one and done.

It is the long-term relationship that builds continuity, smoothness of operation, predictability, and allows you to work on your practice as opposed to in, which in the case of the latter, you are merely an employee, not really a business owner.

These are the five fundamentals of marketing, which, when mastered, can turn an average practice into an unbelievable mountain of wealth.

Here they are:

1. Attract more clients.
2. Sell or cross sell services to existing clients.
3. Increase the average sale to each client.
4. Attract only clients who are a perfect match for you;
5. Recognize that the one thing you have complete control over is yourself—which permits you to build that essential personal client friendship.

You may be asking yourself at this point, "That sounds great, but how do I go about doing these things and taking advantage of these fundamental marketing principles?"

And the answer is...

...keep reading.

SUCCESS
FROM THE INSIDE OUT

Life has no other discipline to impose, if we would but realize it, than to accept life unquestioningly. Everything we shut our eyes to, everything we run away from, everything we deny, denigrate, or despise, serves to defeat us in the end. What seems nasty, painful, evil can become a source of beauty, joy, and strength, if faced with an open mind. Every moment is a golden one for him who has the vision to recognize it as such.

—Henry Miller

Progress Report

If you documented your dream as I suggested on page 16, be sure to periodically check in with yourself and conduct a candid progress report.

If you are working, then there will be progress. Moreover, there will be areas where you have let things slide.

No problem.

INSIDE OUT INSIGHT: You are trying for progress, not for perfection.

Make dates on your calendar over the next twelve months for half-day breaks when you will leave the office and go somewhere relaxing just to think about and work on your dream document.

The more you think about it, the more you will work on it.

Write on a top of a blank page the following question: What do I really want or need to be in order to have my... (insert your dream). Then write down the answer that comes to you, no matter what it is. Then ask yourself the question again (aloud) and record the answer on the same piece of paper. You want to continue to do this until you feel you have exhausted all possibilities.

What have you done? I suggest that you have

tapped into your subconscious mind, the gateway to Universal Intelligence, and you have received inspired thought, upon which you must now act. Just trust in this process with the belief and expectation that you will receive that which you desire.

SUCCESS
FROM THE INSIDE OUT

The world we have created is a product of our thinking; it cannot be changed without changing our thinking.

—Albert Einstein

Hey—Who's In Charge Here, Anyway?

Are you are aware of your thoughts? Most are not. They just come in through your unconscious mind and your emotional/subconscious mind, which controls everything you do, receives them.

I once heard that before Bette Midler goes on stage, she claims she always experiences paralyzing stage fright. However, she has learned that she can neutralize the thoughts of fear of the audience by telling herself that she is the best there is. She says, "I'm the best, I'm the best," which creates a state of mind that allows her to perform. She is rejecting the unwanted thoughts. I suggest that you try it the next time you face a fearful situation.

You can change your state of mind just like that.

At first, the power of choice does not seem very impressive, but as lawyers, we are constantly being "task-diverted" by incoming information. Some call this "urgent trivialities."

The technique you develop is up to you. However, you should know that such technology actually exists.

The power it creates to accomplish your goals is unparalleled.

You become aware you have total control—and once you experience it a few times you will believe in its power. Additionally, you will begin to reject those urgent trivialities, just as you were previously responsible for attracting them because of the energy you put out there. You will be empowering yourself to succeed.

It is amazing what happens in your time and space when you are no longer attracting the urgent trivialities. You have time to think clearly and you act accordingly.

You begin to notice the intuitive and imaginative thoughts—and you can consciously choose them. If you do not, by necessity, you smother all the positive energy with the negative energy *that you mismanaged and let get out of hand.*

Just snap your fingers and stay on the alert for the negative stuff.

You can choke it off before it even begins.

Seven Things You Have to Do Starting Tomorrow Morning

ONE: Purchase, obtain, borrow or otherwise come into possession of Napoleon Hill's classic *Think and Grow Rich* and begin to study it, making certain to read at least some portion every single day. I say this not with the zeal of a religious fanatic, but with the absolute certainty of someone who has benefited from this process.

TWO: Incorporate a fifteen to thirty minute block of time for solitude into your daily schedule. Make this a time when you are free of interruptions and can both relax your mind and focus it on planning how you proceed in the conduct of your career and your life. It is important to include some manner or expression of gratitude about the things life has already given you.

THREE: Acquaint yourself with the mastermind principle and create a mastermind alliance, not only for succeeding at the practice of law, but to enrich the way you live your life.

FOUR: There are many coaches in the realms of goal setting and goal achievement; consider seeking their advice.

Establishing and attaining goals is as much an art and science as anything else. There is a lot more to it than scribbling down a to-do list. It is serious business. Take it seriously.

FIVE: During one of your earliest times of personal solitude, honestly assess—and commit to writing—exactly where you are at that moment. Then, using both imagination and intuition, make a clear decision of exactly where you want to go. Resources and tools to help you accomplish this are readily available. All you have to do is knock.

SIX: Consider attending a seminar or training in which you can become further enlightened about the principles of success. Make certain you attend at least one of these programs annually.

SEVEN: Share with at least one other person what you are learning about success. By doing so, you will come to a higher understanding and awareness—on a much deeper level—of the very information you are attempting to communicate.

The Summation

If it is true—as the principles of success clearly prove—that you are the judge and jury of your own fate, consider this exercise:

Find a quiet place and write down a "summation to the jury" that describes the facts of this case, the precedents upon which your case was constructed, and the rationale that the jury must agree on to find you guilty—beyond a reasonable doubt—of being squarely on the road to succeeding beyond your wildest dreams.

Make this document something you take to heart.

Make it something important.

Do not rush it.

Think about it.

Write it carefully.

Get feed back from a trusted friend or colleague.

Make a summation you can use to fortify yourself in times of trouble and doubt, and make it something you are proud of.

You should be.

It is a description of you as a person, and your dreams and goals and aspirations.

It is a description of your struggle as a human being, reaching far, far beyond the simple length of your arm and grasp, to the stars.

On the other hand, what is a heaven for, anyway?

Now, I have provided a gift for you similar to the one given to me. If there is a magic pill to launch you into the world of success, this may be it. After you have used it, you have my permission to copy it and share it with whomever you choose.

It is your *Power of Attorney*.

Succeeding In the Practice of Law From the Inside Out

Well, I can see we have come full circle.

From a state of being barely aware of centuries old success principles, to having thought about them clearly and carefully in the context of our own lives and careers as attorneys.

I would never want you to forget how we got to this state of affairs, and what we as a profession—and you as an individual—need to do: we need to begin rebuilding this great profession—from the inside out.

About Larry Levin

Larry Levin is a leading legal marketing and development coach who presents to various bar and legal groups on the topics of ethics, professionalism, marketing, goal setting and achievement to show lawyers how to succeed at the practice of law from the inside out. A practicing attorney and senior partner at the law firm Shor, Levin & DeRita in Jenkintown, Pennsylvania, Larry has built his firm into a multi million dollar practice over the past three decades, generating $22 million in sales per year. He began his career out of a rented old barbershop space in 1971, and since then Larry and his partners have used the powerful and practical techniques described in this book to achieve both the personal and professional success that many lawyers dream of. Also dedicated to restoring prestige to the legal profession, Larry directs seminars and teleseminars to lead lawyers in the effort to bring back the trusted professional image they once had, and shed the negative perception that has developed over the years. Larry's articles have been published in leading legal publications and he is past chairman and founder of the Montgomery County Young Lawyers Association; past committee member of the Pennsylvania Disciplinary Board; and founder of 4 Lawyers Only, LLC., coaching lawyers in wealth building and success principles.

If you're ready to take control of your life and your profession to achieve the success and satisfaction that you deserve, Larry invites you to read *Power of Attorney* and realize the guiding principles that will allow you to gain balance and success in all aspects of your life!

FREE!

THE POWER OF ATTORNEY
Your own personal declaration of independence, freedom and fulfillment.

As you know, 'Power of Attorney' is one of the most powerful documents in the legal profession. Put this "power" to work for you. This document will be your personal manifesto of fulfillment. All you have to do is give yourself permission to succeed at the level of your dreams. Suitable for framing, 4 Lawyers Only, LLC has developed this document to empower you to succeed in any and all endeavors. Your success is assured!

Yes! *Send my* FREE *"Power of Attorney" to:*

Name _____

Address _____

City _____ State ____ Zip _____

Email _____

Mail completed form to:

4 Lawyers Only, LLC
261 Old York Road, Suite 200
Jenkintown, PA 19046